MW01047792

Pregnancy is the designed

consequence of sex.

Sex is a music playlist the sexual partners are enjoying together. Either partner can hit the pause or stop button at any point during the song. Either partner can skip a track. But most important, only the partner who hit the button can undo the choice they made.

"No means no"...

violating this simple rule

is rape.

Sex and Pregnancy

It's ludicrous to suggest that any human female in America over the age of 13 does not know that you get pregnant because you have sex.

Male and female genitalia are designed to make babies and with the obvious exception of artificial insemination, every single human pregnancy on this planet, wanted or unwanted, planned or otherwise, is the result of sex between a biological male and a biological female.

Pregnancy is the designed consequence of sex.

But sex which leads to pregnancy is not as simple a topic as it might appear on the surface. Any sexual activity in which one party doesn't give their full consent to begin with, wishes to withdraw their consent after giving it, or is incapable of giving consent in the first place, is rape.

Think of sex as a music playlist the sexual partners are enjoying together. Either partner can hit the pause or stop button at any point during the song. Either partner can skip a track. But most important, only the partner who hit the button can undo the choice they made. If he doesn't like a song, he can choose to skip it and she cannot replay. If she wants to hit pause, only she can hit play again. And that holds true for any song in the playlist, and at any point in the song.

No means no and violating this simple rule is rape.

In the context of a woman's unwanted pregnancy, no matter how unwise or even stupid the choices the woman

A REAL MAN

would never, ever

violate the principle of

"No means No"!

made leading up to sex, no matter how she was dressed, where she went, how she behaved, what attention she invited or encouraged, how drunk or stoned she was, or even if she changed her mind in the middle of sex... if she does not or is unable to give consent, she was raped.

As a side note, I would argue that *a real man would never, ever violate this principle*.
A male who would do so is either still unformed and immature as a real man or broken in some way on the inside.

The woman has the right to choose what happens with and to her own body, and "no means no."

The conversation about abortion must start with a conversation about sex.

Pregnancy is the result of a long list of very simple yes/no choices.

The Right to Choose

Taking this idea one step further, Pro-Choice is rooted in two central dogmas of empowerment... ***The woman has the right to choose what happens with and to her own body, and "no means no."***

Most debate about abortion starts at the point of an unwanted pregnancy. For the most part the debate chooses to limit the conversation to that one single choice... whether or not to abort. But in ***the real context of choice***, abortion is sequentially the last place the conversation should start and the last of a long list of choices in the matter. Pregnancy starts with sex, so ***the conversation about abortion must start with a conversation about sex.***

Here's a key point... every single decision you will ever make answers a yes/no question, and when you think otherwise... you changed the question.

This means that every sex act which culminates in pregnancy ***is the result of a long list of very simple yes/no choices*** by both the male and the female partner. Ego, motive, desire, circumstances and hormones may make the choices very difficult to make, but the choices themselves are simple. Choices made about clothing, location and company can elevate the risk of rape. Choices around drugs and alcohol compromise your ability to make sound choices. The choice to use effective birth control determine the probability of pregnancy. The choice to say "no". The choice to accept a "no". Even the choice to have sex at all.

As with Pregnancy, Abortion is also the result of another long list of very simple yes/no choices.

And after sex there are even more choices. The choice to take a chance on pregnancy. The choice to report a rape to the police. The choice to take immediate pregnancy preventive measures ("morning after" pill). The choice to wait and see if there will be a pregnancy. The choice to abort the pregnancy. The choice of when in the development of the fetus to abort the pregnancy. The fact is, **abortion is the result of another long list of very simple yes/no choices**.

Choice after choice after choice. And every choice has consequences. It doesn't make the slightest difference whether we know what the consequences will be or whether we gripe or moan or beg or weep afterwards... the inescapable laws of the universe have mandated consequences for every decision we make.

Which leads us to *accountability and responsibility*.

Unless she was raped, the woman is completely,

totally and solely to blame for a pregnancy.

The woman has the last word.

Either "no means no"

and she is ultimately responsible

for exercising that right,

or "no doesn't mean no".

Accountability vs Responsibility

We live in a world and culture where individuals struggle to or accept *accountability or responsibility*.

A very simple way to explain the difference is this... you are accountable (to be blamed for the outcome) if it was in your power to materially change the course of what has happened in the past, but you are responsible for (in charge of) making decisions for what will happen in your future. *It is your inescapable duty, your responsibility, to make informed, sensible decisions for your future.*

Consider this statement carefully... where rape was NOT the case, *the woman is completely, totally and solely to blame for pregnancy*. She alone is accountable. No matter what decisions or choices the man made which did not violate the dogma of "no means no", if the woman chose to do nothing to prevent the pregnancy, she alone is accountable (to blame). Why? Because *she has the last word* over what happens to her body. She has the responsibility to make choices. Doing nothing is also a choice, and these choices are her duty, her responsibility, to make.

Recognizing this elemental truth is the ultimate feminine empowerment because it puts all the control in the hands of the woman. Ignoring or refuting it is a cop-out. *Either no means no and she is ultimately responsible for exercising that right, or no does not mean no.* You cannot have it both ways.

Accountability to the past is independent of the responsibility for the future.

After pregnancy it doesn't make any difference who is to blame.

If a woman was not raped and then becomes pregnant it is only because she made a series of choices which ultimately allowed the pregnancy. Even more simply... if she did not make deliberate choices that would be 100% guaranteed to prevent the pregnancy... she chose, even if only by default, to be pregnant.

On the other hand, if her choices were ignored, if she said no and her partner was not man enough to honor her wishes, then he alone is accountable. If he forced her then then he is entirely to blame for the pregnancy.

But *accountability to the past is independent of the responsibility for the future*, and this is where responsibility for the future of that pregnancy comes into play.

This is a simple and inescapable fact... *it doesn't make any difference who is to blame after pregnancy*. Choices were made and the deed was done. But because her body is her own and the potential pregnancy will happen to her body only, she alone has the final say in the choices which will determine the outcome of pregnancy. She has all the power and the man can merely express his preferences. He only has a say if she chooses to allow it. This is the next inescapable responsibility for feminine empowerment.

It takes at least 30 hours after sex before

an egg is fully fertilized by the sperm

to form a Zygote,

the very first genetically complete cell

to contain a complete set of

living human DNA.

The Biology of Pregnancy

This is where it is important to understand a tiny bit more detail about pregnancy, most specifically about the Zygote.

A Zygote is sequentially the very first genetically complete cell to contain a complete set of living human DNA. It is formed after the sperm swims into the fallopian tubes of the woman's body. It is here, and only here, where it responds to the environment and physiologically changes into something capable of penetrating the outer shell of the egg. This takes time. Then it must penetrate the egg. More time. And then the DNA within the sperm and egg must unite into one. Even more time. A Zygote… this single cell with every genetic component it needs to grow, develop and mature at a living cellular level as a human being… does not exist until that process is complete.

Once the Zygote has formed, nothing more is required to sustain life except shelter and sustenance, and these requirements are no different than those of a 2-year-old, 20-year-old or 80-year-old.

But here is the key point in the context of abortion… *it takes at least 30 hours after sex before an egg is fertilized by the sperm to form a Zygote*.

The implications of this fact are huge.

The final decision about that pregnancy,

the final responsibility, is hers alone.

She would be wise to factor in the risk that her

birth control measure is not always completely

successful.

Choices After Sex

A woman has at least 30 hours after sex to prevent pregnancy because it takes a minimum of 30 hours for the Zygote to form! More to the point, she has at least 30 hours to exercise her responsibility. That's 30 hours to decide what she will do about the potential pregnancy. And this is critical... *the final say about that potential pregnancy, the final responsibility, is hers alone*.

In the case where rape was NOT involved, if she believes she and/or her partner have already made sound birth control decisions leading up to this point, she may decide that no further action is necessary. In this case she would be wise to factor in the risk that *birth control measures are not always completely successful*. The fact is that there are varying degrees of risk pregnancy associated with different birth control methods, so there may always be a risk if she chooses *not to say no* to sex.

On the other hand, she may be concerned that the risk of pregnancy is unacceptably high. She may know she had no birth control measures in place, or that there was a gap in her birth control effort. She may even worry that the birth control efforts failed somehow. At this point she has both the choice *and the time* to use the "morning after" pill to prevent any chance of the Zygote forming. This would mean no abortion would be necessary!

On the other hand, she may also make a far less responsible decision... to take a chance on the outcome.

After the long list of choices preceding

pregnancy, she only has two remaining choices

once the Zygote has formed...

to carry to term, or abort.

Despite bad choices, poor planning or the failed execution of any birth control strategy she may have, she may still choose to do no more than hope nothing happens. At this point, if she becomes pregnant, she chose pregnancy by default.

In the case where rape was involved, the only difference in the available choices around pregnancy is whether she chooses to go to a hospital and report the rape to the police. It seems obvious to assume that she would choose to report the rape, but it is a well-documented and sad fact that this is not always the case. However, if she does, the hospital will provide the "morning after" pill and the potential pregnancy would be prevented… and the option of abortion would never even come up.

After all these scenarios, if she becomes pregnant, her choices can only be one of two things… to carry to term, or abort.

An abortion would only be necessary if the woman CHOSE NOT to go to a hospital and report the rape.

Reasons for Abortion

Over the years the Guttmacher Institute has asked thousands of women why they chose to abort their pregnancy. Every single reason given can be summarized into four categories... finances, career/work, timing or health. Surprisingly, these reasons were essentially the same no matter how far along the pregnancy was at the time of abortion.

The research goes on to highlight the impact poverty, broken family units and race/ethnicity has on abortion rates.

A relatively miniscule proportion of abortions are to terminate pregnancies to save the life of a mother in imminent danger of harm or death. In fact, the need for this is incredibly rare since in most cases the risk to the mother can be medically managed until the pregnancy is far enough along to safely remove a living, viable baby from the womb for a successful, living birth.

Just as minuscule is the proportion of abortions to terminate pregnancies caused by rape. In this case, an abortion would only be necessary if the woman ***CHOSE NOT to go to a hospital and report the rape***. If she had, the ER would have given her the option of taking the morning after pill to prevent the pregnancy. But because she chose not go to the hospital, because she chose not to report a rape, she chose by default to allow a pregnancy.

According to a detailed survey by the

Guttmacher Institute,

mothers choose abortion to satisfy

their personal preferences

or perceived needs.

The proportion of pregnancies aborted because the fetus is deemed at risk of some abnormality is also tiny and is predicated on one of two reasons. Either the mother does not feel up to the challenge of raising an "abnormal" child, or she decides on behalf of the child that the quality of life for that child would be unbearable for the child. This decision is made without considering that, in almost all cases, when these children are allowed to live and thrive, they are grateful for and enjoy the life they have and would NOT choose to have never lived.

No matter what reasons women give for their abortion, however, they all have one common theme... ***Mothers choose abortion to satisfy their personal preferences or perceived needs.***

And most often they justify doing so by claiming their inalienable right of physical self-determination... their right to control what happens to their body and when.

"We hold these truths to be self-evident, that all men are created equal, that they are endowed by their Creator with certain unalienable rights, that among these are Life, Liberty, and the Pursuit of Happiness…"

Our "inalienable rights" have a Hierarchy of Merit.

My right to pursue happiness does not trump your right to freedom.

And my right to freedom does not trump your right to life.

Our "Inalienable Rights" vs Role of Law

"We hold these truths to be self-evident, that all men are created equal, that they are endowed by their Creator with certain unalienable rights, that among these are Life, Liberty, and the Pursuit of Happiness..."

Legislation has already determined that the phrase "all men" does not exclude women, and also permits no differentiation by race, color, religion, sex or any other. Further, these rights were listed within the text of the Declaration of Independence in that specific hierarchical order... Life, Liberty, and the Pursuit of Happiness... for two reasons.

First, it is an exercise of the most fundamental existential logic. A single human being cannot have liberty without life and cannot pursue happiness without freedom to do so.

Second, it defines a hierarchy of merit.

My right to pursue happiness does not trump your right to freedom. Thousands of Americans, primarily Republicans, died during the Civil War in support of this statement as they fought to end slavery in America. The right of a slave owner to take freedom from another in support of a lifestyle which celebrated their pursuit of happiness has long been outlawed in America. Similarly, we have child sex trafficking laws in place intended to prevent pedophiles from inflicting their unwelcome quest for twisted pleasure on helpless children.

A society built solely on the idea that every member may exercise their rights without the restraints of law is anarchy.

Law-abiding citizens choose to selectively limit or relinquish their rights for the greater good of our society.

Similarly, my right to freedom does not trump your right to life. There is no constitutional right for me to kill you in the name of any of the five freedoms guaranteed by the first amendment (religion, speech, press, assembly and petition). There is no law that permits me to kill you just so that I may exercise my right to freedom of speech. On the contrary, my sole recourse if you prevent me from exercising my right to freedom of speech is a court of law, not murder.

Think about it. *A society built solely on the idea that every member may exercise their rights without the restraints of law is anarchy.*

When you boil it all down, we legislate to prevent the foolish, the illogical, and the selfish among us from violating the hierarchy of rights and thereby infringing on the rights of others. These laws define how we exercise our "inalienable rights" as human beings living in a healthy, peaceful society.

By accepting lives not rooted in anarchy, law-abiding citizens choose to ***selectively*** limit or relinquish some of their rights for the greater good of our society. More than that, we demand that those who do not accept these restraints be punished by the law. This is entirely appropriate and logical.

Granted, too much law places too much power into the hands of a small ruling class and eventually strips us of all our rights. In fact, it was for this exact reason America declared war and embarked on a costly quest for independence from the King. It's also why our Founding Fathers wrote the Declaration of Independence and the Constitution to form our Constitutional Republic. It was

The practical and inevitable outcome of allowing every single human being to pursue everything that makes them happy immediately and without consequence paves the way to anarchy and tyranny.

Fact: Some humans delight to varying degrees in the pain and misery of others, to the point of rape, torture and murder.

the reason they chose to separate the powers of the Executive, Legislative and Judicial branches. It was the reason for the electoral college. And it was why the right to bear arms was written as the Second Amendment.

Some might argue against the idea that choosing to abide by the reasonable law of the land is the Ying to the Yang of personal liberty, but the practical and inevitable outcome of allowing every single human being to pursue everything that makes them happy immediately and without consequence paves the way to tyranny, oppression, violence, horror and death. To put it another way, when someone exercises their right to happiness without restraint, they will inevitably trespass over the rights to life and liberty of someone else.

For the doubters, here's a case in point.

Fact: Some humans delight to varying degrees in the misery of others. This is a well-known phenomenon represented in a broad spectrum, from bullies to serial killers. At their extremes, these twisted people revel in torturing, raping and killing.

How does society react to these people? We classify them as Sociopaths and Psychopaths. We may vilify them, be entertained by them (Dexter, anyone?), or make movies and video games to profit on the curious capacity of humans to explore these dark fantasies vicariously. Furthermore, if the success of endless documentaries on the topic is any indication, at the very least we find them morbidly fascinating.

Granted, known psychopaths who have tortured, raped and killed in their twisted pursuits of happiness are relatively rare in modern times, but if we were to remove

We perceive others on a sliding scale. On one end is love, and on the other is hate.

We all recognize the need for laws and consequences that will keep stronger, greedier or more violent people from impinging on the personal rights of others.

the consequences, far more people would choose to explore these fantasies in real life. Doing so vicariously through video games will no longer be enough. Without law, without consequence, absolutely nothing will prevent more and more people from pursuing pleasure and happiness at a horrific cost to others.

We perceive others on a sliding scale. On one end is love and on the other is hate.

For those we love, we limit our generosity based on how selfishly we manage the resources by which we can express generosity. For those we hate, we restrain our expressions of hatred to the extent we fear the consequences. We are afraid of the consequences we believe will follow when we violate certain standards of behavior, whether we support those standards or not.

While we like to think altruism is the guiding light for all people, the reality is that we all recognize the need for laws and consequences that will keep stronger, greedier or more violent people from impinging on our own personal rights.

Selfishly, while we demand laws restraining the "extreme" efforts of others to pursue their rights, most of us to one extent or another resist the same laws when they restrain our own behavior. And before you challenge that statement, how do you think most people react to a speeding fine?

The embarrassing truth is that human beings typically only demand laws that protect their own selfish interests,

We have to understand

who qualifies under the Law

for protection of the

"inalienable right" to life.

and expect those laws to include consequences that are strictly enforced... on others.

Still doubting? How many people who are guilty of murder stand up in court, unprompted, and admit guilt? How often do people acknowledge guilt without prompting or reservation, own it, and then stand ready, without challenge, to accept the consequences?

Life, Liberty, and the Pursuit of Happiness... without law protecting the hierarchy of these rights and thereby framing a safe, peaceful society, our unrestrained, selfish grasping for happiness will inevitably pave the way to anarchy, destruction and misery.

Criminalizing murder, for example, restricts the socially defined extremes of our personal liberty and establishes severe consequences for taking the life of another living human being.

In context then, we must thoroughly understand who qualifies for the protection under the law for their "inalienable right" to life.

The single most important issue in in answering this question revolves around one question and one question only...

When is a human?

Is a viable "preemie" able to survive as a human being with "inalienable rights"?

The Debate of Human Life

The single most important issue in answering this question revolves around one question and one question only... ***When is a human?***

The answer to this question defines the debate in America. Is it the sperm and egg? Moment of sex? Point of fertilization? Some level of growth and development? Viability outside the womb?

Within the context of religion, ultra-conservative Christians have classified the viable sperm or egg of a human as the start of human life. These same people are likely to argue against all forms of birth control.

Another group of believers may argue that human life starts after sex.

In either case, they believe God plays one of three critical roles. First, God decides the outcome of each sexual act. Second, God designed a process which, by design, causes pregnancy according to odds influenced by the design of the male and female body. And third, God may be petitioned in prayer to change what may have been a previously "determined" outcome.

Weaving in and out of the religious perspective are various questions of science.

Does a "viable" baby get "inalienable rights" and, if so, how do we define "viable"? Is viability the ability to sustain life and, if so, is viability constrained by the effort required of others to sustain that life? Do we use as our baseline a

The leap from "too young to keep alive" to "too sick or old to keep alive" is a very small leap deeper into barbarism.

More liberal proponents of Pro-Choice

now claim that a viable child

capable of life and already outside the womb

is only granted the rights of a human being

if the mother chooses to allow it!

development stage, arbitrarily measured in weeks, the presence of a heartbeat, or the ability to respond to some stimulus?

It wasn't that long ago that we changed the point of viability from 28 weeks to 21 weeks based on the ability of medicine to sustain the life of a "preemie" after birth. Then when we chose to move the number from 28 to 21, thereby admitting that our arbitrary definition is flawed because medicine is aggressively working to move that marker, even to the point where artificial incubation is a success!

Using the flawed criterium built around the concept of a development stage, we buy into the idea that a child may be granted the rights of a living human being only contingent on the *ever-changing limitations* of NICU medicine and science.

The more liberal proponents of Pro-Choice now claim that *despite viability, a birthed child should only be granted the rights of a human being if the mother chooses to allow it.*

As a related side note, what if we were to say that the viability of a human being is diminished to the point of losing their rights to life if they have a cancer medicine cannot yet cure? Similarly, what if a human being were to relinquish their right to life because they get too old for science and medicine to economically keep alive?

The leap from "too young to keep alive" to "too sick or old to keep alive" is a very small leap into barbarism.

The only things a Zygote lacks are

shelter and nutrition

from a responsible caregiver...

no different than the needs of

a three-month-old baby.

There is one starting point that is both biologically clear and vastly inconvenient to the Pro-Choice argument... DNA.

There are two pertinent and undeniable facts of science... life exists even at the single-cell level, and DNA determines if an organism is or was human based on the 23 pairs of chromosomes which define homo sapiens.

Medically speaking, when 23 chromosomes from a sperm unites with the 23 chromosomes from an egg to form a single-celled zygote, that single cell is both alive and human.

Not only that, that Zygote possesses every, single thing it needs to develop and grow into a college graduate... except one... ***shelter and nutrition from a responsible caregiver, and this is no different than the needs of a three-month-old baby***. In fact, it's usually much easier physically to carry a baby in the womb before it is viable than it is to take care of it after birth.

All that said, how are the rights of the mother properly balanced with those of the child?

By law, Americans have suspended

the consequences of killing a human being

whose rights are otherwise

explicitly protected by law

under three circumstances...

War, self-defense and the death penalty.

Rights of Mother vs Baby

This is where the "inalienable right" of every living human being intersects with how the law contextually defines a living human being.

In order to legally terminate the life inside the womb, we must do one of two things. Either we legally expand on what constitutes and exception to murder, or we legislate a definition of human life which excludes science.

By law, Americans have suspended the consequences of terminating the life of a human being whose rights have otherwise been protected by law under three circumstances... War, self-defense and the death penalty.

The fact that *war* is a legal permission to murder under certain circumstances (defined to a large extent by the Geneva Code) is well documented and understood.

Where the laws of *self-defense* permit deadly force to protect life and property (however that threat may be defined from state to state), choosing to threaten the life and possessions of someone else is, by default, a choice to surrender your right to life.

By the same token, the *death penalty* has been established in some states as the legal consequence when one human being kills another in some particularly horrific or pre-meditated fashion. Choosing an act that has the death penalty as a consequence is also, by default, a choice to surrender your right to life.

By claiming within the law that

the entity alive in the womb

is not human under the law,

we fall into the same mindset as

Nazis and American slave owners.

If we accept that the entity living within the

womb is a human being, we have absolutely no

grounds for allowing the murder of these

innocents.

The fact that death as consequence is not applied in every instance makes the risk seem acceptable to some. But playing the odds does not eliminate the chance of death, it simply makes it more likely that some will take the chance.

War, self-defense and the death penalty are legally permitted exceptions to the right to life specifically when a competent, functioning, reasoning adult has egregiously broken with the rules of society, knew and understood the consequences, and chose to break the rules anyway. They are not innocent.

But abortion, the term used to describe the murder of the unborn, is very, very different.

To justify abortion, either the law defines a living entity comprised of human DNA as a non-human life, or the law allows a mother to rank her "pursuit of happiness" over the life of a helpless, *innocent* human being.

In either case the law has historically proven itself to be fallible.

By claiming within the law that a fetus of whatever viability is not human under the law, we are allowing ourselves to fall into the same mindset as Nazis and American slave owners, and the Bill of Rights has already addressed this evil.

On the other hand, if we accept that the entity living within the womb is a human being, there are no legitimate grounds for prioritizing the very selfish pursuit of happiness over life by allowing the murder of these innocents.

By virtue of the long list of choices she made,

the mother by default CHOSE pregnancy,

and by default CHOSE to subjugate

her right to pursue happiness

to the right of the child to live.

Just as no one-year old infant has chosen to violate the rights of another human being, these children are blameless. Just as no one-year-old can defend itself, these children are defenseless. And just as no one-year-old has been given the choice to be there, these children are alive because an adult made a series of choices that culminated in the existence of this child.

By virtue of the long list of choices she made, **the mother by default chose pregnancy and by default chose to subjugate her right to pursue happiness to the right of the child to live.**

Whatever her personal, selfish or cowardly preferences may be, no matter how she may twist or distort her perception of value, the law must follow the precedents of the Bill of Rights and prioritize the right of the fetus to life over the selfish right of the mother to pursue happiness.

Roe vs Wade did not rule

on the legality of abortion.

The Supreme Court very deliberately

sought to avoid mandating

what constituted

"the potentiality of human life".

State vs Federal Law

The intent of our founding fathers in the design of our government was that the states should govern themselves, and federal law would only take precedence in a very limited capacity.

Our Government today has largely forgotten that, just as they have forgotten the true role of the Legislature.

But one of the fundamental areas where Federal law trumps State laws relates to human rights. No state may legislate in a manner that restricts the rights and civil liberties of any human being more than what federal law allows.

And that was the basis of Roe vs Wade.

Roe vs Wade did not rule on the legality of abortion. This myth is commonly screamed and shrieked as dogma. In reality, Roe vs Wade stated that the constitutional right to privacy extends to a woman's decision to have an abortion. However, Roe vs Wade still provided provision for the State to regulate abortion "to protect women's health ***and the potentiality of human life***" provided the State did not unfairly limit access to abortions that may otherwise be deemed by the state to be legal.

Along with subsequent rulings, the Supreme Court in Roe vs Wade deliberately avoided mandating what constituted "the potentiality of human life" in the context of a pregnancy. That's not to say the Court did not make suggestions in the context of viability, but they stopped short of making a definitive ruling one way or another.

Every single state still has the legal right to limit

abortion based on how they define a viable (or

potentially viable) human being whose rights

should be protected under the law.

This in part is why the Pro-Choice camp

reacts with such vigor and vitriol

at the slightest threat to Roe vs Wade...

they know it is vulnerable.

The structure of the decision made in Roe vs Wade has long been lamented in legal circles, and opinion varies on just how defensible the ruling truly is in the context of "the potentiality of human life".

This means that *every single state still has the legal right to limit abortion to any extent they see fit based on how they define a viable (or potentially viable) human being whose inalienable right to life must be protected under the law*.

Since the Supreme Court has not yet definitively ruled on when is a living human, States may continue to define this for themselves and New York, in fact, did just that. They claim that the human DNA living and growing within the womb is not human and therefore has no rights under the law. Just as the Nazis did with Jews. Just as slave owners did with African slaves.

Similarly, conservative states have chosen to legislate in the opposite direction, further setting the stage for a legal challenge to make it to the Supreme Court.

This inherent vulnerability of Roe vs Wade of is why Pro-Choice proponents react with such vigor and vitriol at the slightest threat to their perceived right to abortion.

Only negative consequences

prevent the more harmful expressions

of our free will.

Humans love to live life in the loopholes.

We rebel against the intent of the law.

Impact of Law

The idea of free will is that we may choose to do absolutely whatever we want personally. But the way man has treated man throughout history proves that, without laws and consequences, our selfishness and greed absolutely guarantee we will trample on the rights of humans around us. Almost without fail, we lie, cheat, steal and murder to satisfy our own desires to the extent we feel we can escape consequence.

Only negative consequences prevent the more harmful expressions of our free will.

Human nature also tends towards ignoring the spirit (or intent) of the law and following the letter of the law instead... and then only if the perceived consequences to breaking the law are greater than the perceived benefits.

When elected legislators get it right, the laws are an expression of the majority view, are designed for the greater good of the majority, establish the least possible constraint to free will, and close as many loopholes used to evade the intent as possible.

The great weakness to legal obedience is that laws often require interpretation to address unforeseen gaps in the letter of the law. Why? Because ***we love to live life in the loopholes***.

When law infringes on how we want to express our free will, we resist. ***We rebel against the intent of the law***. We demand clarification on the exact letter of the law so

A precedent becomes the excuse

which begins a cascade of court rulings

leading us further and further away

from the original intent of the law.

that we can still get as much of what we want without consequences.

Loosely written laws designed to address most cases often do not clarify how the law should address the exception. The nature of the individual is to seek greater freedom to satisfy personal needs, wants or desires, balking against the constraints of law. Consequently, when we stand accused of breaking the original, broader law, we go to court looking for a well-meaning judge to rule the exception in our favor. No matter how well-meaning the intent of the judge, or how miniscule the shift away from the original, broad text of the law, any final ruling on an exception becomes a precedent for future rulings on exception.

Put another way, a legal precedent is an earlier decision used as a guide in subsequent similar circumstances… and this is where the slope gets slippery.

In many ways a precedent becomes the excuse which begins a cascade of court rulings leading us further and further away from the original intent of the law.

And so you reach the point where murder, the unlawful killing of another human being without legal justification, is rare while killing is common.

Nowhere is this more obvious than abortion.

Science says our 23 pairs of chromosomes define us as human, and further claims that a single cell existing as a unicellular organism, even if existing only briefly, is alive. Therefore, at a purely scientific level, a Zygote has "the potentiality of human life" if provided the shelter and

The state of New York has essentially ruled that "the potentiality of human life" exists only if the mother chooses to allow that life, even after the child is viable outside the womb.

The unprecedented genocide of infants across all States on America will only end when the Supreme Court rules on when we are human under the law.

sustenance of the womb, no different than a one-year-old has "the potentiality of human life" as long as it is given shelter and sustenance.

But precedent follows precedent, which is why the state of New York has now essentially ruled that "the potentiality of human life", even after the child is viable outside the womb, exists only if the mother chooses to allow that life.

This is not a view shared by the vast majority of our nation, but without a definitive ruling by the Supreme Court to the contrary, there is nothing to prevent what is largely considered infanticide. Not just that, there now exists no legal reason why the deliberate killing of an unborn child, even within the womb of a mother desperate to have the baby, would not be ruled as no more than damage to the property of the woman.

The unprecedented genocide of infants across all States in America will only end when the Supreme Court rules on when we are human and our right to life becomes protected under the Bill of Rights.

Made in the USA
Middletown, DE
17 August 2022